Contents

INTRODUCTION

A silenced mouth is silenced destiny. Whatever you say is what you will have. If [l]? challenges can get you to be quiet or negative about yourself, it will be hard to fulfil Go[d] destiny for your life. There is power in our thoughts, If God cannot change your thoug[ht] process, he won't be able to change your life.

The way you see life determines a lot about the way you would live that life. A weak thoug[ht] will produce a weak word, a weak word will produce a weak destiny. When you think sma[ll] you will talk small and do small things. As a man thinks, so is he. If God can get a hold [of] your mind, then he can alter your thinking pattern and you will begin to see differently.

A renewed mind is a renewed life, your mind is very important to God. Nothing will change your life until you change your mind. The quality of your thought will determine the quality [of] your words. Do you wonder why Jesus was unique? Why Jesus was able to fulfil h[is] destiny? Everything was different about him. The secret was his mindset, he had a ri[ch] mindset, that's why he could manufacture money from the mouth of a fish.

Jesus was innovative, never repeated the same miracle the same way, he came up with ne[w] ideas of solving problems for people around him. Jesus knew the power of words, so [he] always says what God the father wanted. He silenced the storm by his word. Many of us ju[st] speak without understanding the power of words.

It is important to remember the power of faith is in action. If we truly believe God, we need [to] act on his word and trust him to always show up in time of troubles. Jesus always acted [on] God's word, and he used the word of God to silence the devil when he was tempted.

Think and speak positively is compilation of positive confession received from the lord ov[er] many years of serving him. It is a 21-day teaching and positive mind building journey wi[th] over 210 positive confessions. Shared with many personal insights to empower you fig[ht] through life challenges and come out a victor.

This 21-day interactive devotional journal immerses you into a positive atmosphere whe[re] you can begin to see possibility where you have been experiencing difficulties. Th[is] devotional will reveal the power of thought, the power of speaking positively and the pow[er] of action on God's word.

CHAPTER 1

Words Are Powerful

ords are powerful because they shape our world. Every person on this planet has the wer to shape their own destinies by their words. We paint a picture of our lives through our rds. There is power in what we say, and we can either make our lives better or worse ough what we say.

e scripture tells us how God spoke the world into existence (Genesis 1:3) "God said let ere be light and there was light". The first thing that was created apart from the heaven and e earth in the beginning was light. The interesting part was that the light was spoken into istence, before it appeared. There are many good things that would not happen in our es until we beginning to call them forth.

e scripture tells us in (1 John 1:5) "This is the message we have heard from him and oclaim to you, that God is light and in him is no darkness at all."

en though God is light when he created the heaven and the earth, the earth was without m and void, and darkness was on the face of the deep. God still had to deliberately call th light for darkness to depart. This shows that whatever greatness you carry on the inside ll not manifest in the physical until you call it forth. God established a principle here, that at you decree is what you will have.

nazing, God full of light still had to call forth light. Many people are carrying greatness in em, but this greatness won't manifest if they are not intentional about calling their eatness forth. Your words are powerful, words are the raw material God used to create the rld. (Hebrews 11:3) "By Faith we understand that the worlds were framed by the word of d, so that the things which are seen were not made of things which are visible" So the rld we see today was called into existence by God's word. Since we were created in d's nature, man also took the same ability from God's nature, directly or indirectly man s called all kinds of things into existence.

you are going to have a positive shift in life, it's necessary that you speak positively. You ed to recognise the power of confession and believe you have the power in your mouth to ange your world whether physically, spiritually, financially, and mentally. If you speak the ht words, you can change your life. Your words are powerful. "Whatever you believe and y consistently will eventually become your reality.

Day 1

(Positive Confession)

1. I am blessed and highly favoured.
2. I am a light in the darkness, I shine bright and brighter in Jesus' name.
3. God's glory radiates upon my life.
4. I am healed, Jesus took my sickness and pain away.
5. I can never be poor, I am rich. Christ became poor so that I might be rich.
6. I am Justified, I am glorified, no shame in my life.
7. My shame is taken away, my pain is healed in his name.
8. It's my season of fruitfulness, I can never be barren.
9. It's my time to shine, all things are working for my good.
10. The earth is working in my favour.
11. Nothing can stop me, there's no mountain I cannot move by faith in Christ Jesus.
12. I am powerful, I carry God's grace upon my life.

CHAPTER 2

Watch What You Say

is important to watch the words that come out of our mouth. As we have established a nciple which shows that we create our own world by the words of our mouth. So therefore, at means whatever we are currently seeing in our lives are a result of the words of our outh.

ou can either create a positive environment or a negative situation for yourself by what you y. So, watch what you have been saying. Many use words like I can't make it, success is t for people like us, every time we pronounce words like that the devil is happy because e have just given him something to use against us.

e scripture says in (Proverbs 18:21) "Death and life are in the power of the tongue and ose who love it will eat its fruits" The book of truth is telling us there is power to create life d death in our tongue.

ou can either call life or death into your life by opening your mouth to speak. Watch what u say, erase negative words and negative pronunciations from your life. Watch what you e calling into existence.

ere is power in what you say, you may not see what you have said immediately because e scripture says the words we speak are like seeds, they start in a small form until they ow into trees and then trees grow to become a big forest.

ery time you say a negative word you are sowing a seed. The scripture says Death and e are in the power of the tongue those who love it will eat the fruits, which means everyone all bear the consequences of their own words.

These means whatever you sow with your mouth, that you will reap. God cannot be mock for whatsoever a man soweth, that shall he also reap (Gal 6:7). Every time you say wor like you are small, you are poor, you are limited, you are sowing a negative seed into yc life.

So, watch what you are saying, watch what you are sowing into your life because very so those seeds will eventually produce fruit with consequences you have to bear. Every tir you speak right and use positive words you are sowing a positive seed into your futu "Your words have the power to transform your future. Choose to speak right.

Day 2
(Positive Confession)

1. Arise and Shine, my light has come (Is 60:1)
2. I step into promotion; I step into my next level.
3. Helpers of destiny arise and come to my help.
4. Everything I have lost; I take it back in double folds.
5. My Glory Arise and shine, my glory come out of darkness.
6. I am wealthy, blessed, I am rich, I can never be poor.
7. I receive my joy, my miracles, my heart be filled with joy.
8. Kings shall minister to me; foreigners shall build my walls.
9. I am favoured, I am a product of God's mercy.
10. My gates shall be opened, it shall not be shut.
11. My destiny is glorious, my destiny will not be aborted.
12. I am an eternal excellence, the spirit of excellence is upon me, everything I do becomes excellent.
13. No more affliction, I enter my rest.
14. I Arise, I manifest glory.
15. I am a joy of many generations.
16. I walk out of confusion, shame, and disgrace.
17. I walk out of depression and frustration in the name of Jesus.

CHAPTER 3

VISIBLE TO INVISIBLE

The scripture says the visible world, was not created by the visible things. (Hebrews 11:3) In the beginning God called the world into existence by the word of his mouth. Words cann be seen, they are invisible, however the spiritual principle is that everything we see tod. were called into existence. In Genesis chapter 1:3 God called light into existence, then t light became visible, that shows us that words are the connection between our physic world and the invisible world.

The problem with some people is that they find it hard to operate in two worlds at the sar time, some people don't even believe in the invisible world because they don't see it. T truth is that God created us to operate in two worlds, that why God created man as a spirit a physical body.

What do you want to see in your life, what dreams do you have, what good things have ye imagined, you have the power to convert them to the visible world. All your dreams ar vision are created in the invisible world, they are unseen. For you to be able to bring the into the visible you need to convert them by conceptualising them in your mind and declarir them with your mouth.

No matter the dreams and great imaginations you have in your mind, until you speak and a on them, they will remain in the invisible world. If you want those great dreams to I manifested, you need to speak and say it out, call them forth. Everything I hav accomplished in my life presently are a result of things I said many years ago, especially tl things God told me he will do in my life. When I tell people about them some laugh at me doubt and unbelief even my own friends and family find it hard to believe it. Today, most what I said has come to pass, I am already saying new things. One day a close relative mine say to me, did you know that all the things you said you will become as come to pas except for one, and I smiled.

Many years ago, I discovered a funny spiritual principle in one of the books I read, in th book the person took a picture of a house that he wanted and stuck the picture on the wa After some time, he got that kind of house, and a car that was in the picture of that hous He said when he decided to buy a car, he had a particular car in his mind but at the point deciding he changed his mind when he found this car, unknowing to him that, the car f

ally chose was the car that was parked outside the house of the picture he stuck on his
ll. Later he discovered that was same car and he amazed.

er reading this story I went and cut some pictures from magazine and I pasted them on
wall my years ago, today, almost all of them have come to pass and more, God even did
yond my expectation. Start saying what God told you, don't worry about those mocking
d laughing at you. Until men mock you for declaring what God told you, God won't make
u. Let them mock you, God will make you.

ay what you want to see. The scripture says you shall say a thing and it shall be
tablished unto thee; (Job 22:23). Your words are the raw materials that create your world,
u can call your dreams into reality from the invisible world into the visible world.

ords cannot be seen; words are invisible that's why the bible says in Hebrews 11:3b "so
at the things which are seen were not made of the things which are visible." So, words are
visible, but they carry the power to create things in the physical world. The word of God in
ur mouth, is as powerful as the word of God from God's mouth.

God's word brought the world into existence so also can the word of God bring your
mmand into existence. The bible says in (John 1:1) in the beginning was the word, and the
rd was with God and the word was God. Verse 2:" All things were made through him, that
eans that all the things which we see today were made through the word of God and
thout him nothing was made. God's word in your mouth is a creative force, create your
ure today by confessing God's word.

Day 3

Positive Confession

1. My head, you are meant for Glory.
2. I shall be the head and not the tail.
3. I shall be honoured before those that have mocked me.
4. I walk in dominion; I walk into victory.
5. I shall not lose the battle to the devil.
6. I overcome physically, spiritually, materially and in all areas of my life by the blood of Jesus.
7. I decree and declare that I am a winner in life and in destiny.
8. My head receive power to be lifted.
9. I will not be a figure head in my family.
10. The oil of anointing is upon my head for Favor.

CHAPTER 4

WORDS ARE DYNAMIC

nd the word became flesh and dwelt amongst us, and we beheld his glory, the glory as of e only begotten of the father, full of grace and truth. (John 1:14) The scripture reveals that e word became flesh. God was establishing a principle in this verse of the scripture. There a revelation in this chapter that I got after reading and mediating for some time, one day s scripture opened in a unique way.

od's word which is invisible was spoken to virgin Mary, and it became a force in the ysical realm that she became pregnant without human effort. Wow, that's power, God's rd penetrated the human physical body and formed a physical entity in Mary womb. The isible word by the power of the holy spirit, found its way into Mary's womb and formed a ild, not the child of anybody but of God. God bypassed every human principle of production because he is God.

e word of God is so power that it creates physical realities, the invisible word transformed a baby and the child grew to be the saviour of the word. Simply put the invisible became sible, the spiritual became physical. Your blessings are first spiritual before they become ysical. So, you are not poor, you are just in the process of converting your spiritual essing into the physical.

od's word is so powerful and dynamic, it can't be stopped, it cannot be destroyed by man. od's word outlives every man, God's word is full of creativity, it can bring anything you cree into the physical realm.

ow, this is the amazing part, if the word can become flesh, it can become anything. If you e poor today, if you can get the revelation of God's word about blessings, you can convert e word into real wealth and blessings, if you are sick the word can become your healer, e word of God can become whatever you need in Life. God said to Moses, my name is the I AM THAT I AM, which means God cannot be limited. God is saying, I am whatever you need me to be at any point in time.

God's word can create your future, blessings, money, riches, power, miracles, and lot more. What you need is to know what God's word is saying concerning you. God's word is creative force in your mouth, it can deliver you, it can heal your body, it can change your circumstances for good.

Keep declaring what God has said concerning you in his word. God cannot lie, what he said concerning you will manifest in the physical. You shall see his word come to pass in your life.

(Num 23:19) "God is not a man that he should lie, nor a son of man, that he should change his mind. Has he said, and will he not do? Or has he spoken, and will he not make it good? Whatever God has said he is able to fulfil it.

(Positive Confession)

1. My words are law. Whatever I say will come to pass.
2. Miracles are happening in my life.
3. My season of wonders have come.
4. I enter my season of miracles.
5. I shall be a wonder unto those around me.
6. I am anointed for signs, miracles, and wonders.
7. I receive my miracles now by faith.
8. I download my miracles from the spirit realm into the physical.
9. My miracle manifest now.
10. It's my time for a miracle, I claim that which belongs to me now.

CHAPTER 5

WHAT YOU SAY IS WHAT YOU GET

You can never rise above the level of your confession. The quality of your life is direc[t] linked to the quality of the words that comes out of your mouth. (Job 22:28) "you will al[so] declare a thing, and it will be established for you, so light will shine on your ways. T[he] degree of your establishment in life is connected to the degree of your decree.

The message bible version says you will decide what you want, and it will happen. What y[ou] say is what you get. You can't continue saying negative statement and expect a positi[ve] outcome, that is an error. The scripture says you will decide what you want. So, what do y[ou] want? What have you been deciding about your life? If you want positive things in your li[fe] you must decide it and say the right words, irrespective of what is happening around you.

Your words can change your feelings and your environment. Have you ever noticed th[at] some people are anointed for demoralising the atmosphere with their negative words. If y[ou] are not strong, they can make you have a bad day with their bad words. Some will ma[ke] statement like "am just experiencing a bad day" early in the morning when the day is ju[st] starting off.

The worst part is that they don't keep it to themselves they share and spread their negati[ve] feelings. If you are not careful you also start feeling low, as a child of God you must lea[rn] how to change what you feel, at that moment by speaking positively.

Remember, as a child of the kingdom you must speak strength instead of weakness, spe[ak] life instead of death, speak favour instead of hardship, despite what you feel. You cann[ot] control what people will say around you, but you decide what you want to see in your life a[nd] what you want around you. Your decree is the key to decide what you want, and it w[ill] happen for you. Your words can change your surroundings and your atmosphere anytim[e] anywhere.

DAY 5

(Positive Confession)

1. All things are working for my good
2. I am not a failure, I cannot fail.
3. When I fall, I shall rise again.
4. I am like the eagle; I soar above the storm.
5. Jesus never failed; I will never fail.
6. I am a success; success is my name.
7. Everything is working for my favour.
8. I can never be stranded because my God cannot be stranded.
9. Jesus is the way; he makes way for me.
10. I command whatever that was not working for me before, start working now.

CHAPTER 6

THINK RIGHT

The reason many people cannot speak right is because they don't think right. When t mind is weak, the words coming out of that mouth will be weak. A weak thinking pattern v only produce weak words. "The quality of your words can never be better than the quality your thoughts". (Proverbs 23:7) says "For as he thinks in his heart, so is he. As a man thin so he speaks and act. The quality of your thought will decide the quality of your words. S therefore it is clear that there is a strong connection between man's thought process a what comes out of his mouth.

When you have an overwhelming feeling, you will express it in your words. (Mattew 12:3 says" Out of the abundance of the heart the mouth speaks". Jesus was saying that a go person, out of the good treasure of his heart produces good, and the evil person out of h evil treasure produces evil, for out of the abundance of the heart his mouth speaks. (Lu 6:45). Are you filled with good treasures? Is your heart filled with faith, love, joy, goodnes wisdom, grace, and kindness?

Your mouth will speak what is dominant in your heart, so it important to fill our hearts w faith and God's word. If you are going to ever speak right, you need to be filled with faith God. If you can change your mind, you can change your words, and your life will experien a positive change.

Watch what goes into your heart, what do you mediate upon? Whatever goes into your hea as the power to form the foundation of your belief. God's word is the key to change yo thinking system, if you are going to switch from negative thinking pattern, you need to abso God's word into your mind to override the negative strongholds.

ese negative strongholds are words that have penetrated our minds due to our past periences of failure and disappointment, poor societal culture and limitation, family ckgrounds, slavery, and mediocre mentality.

fore God can change your words, he needs to get a hold of your mind, to input a new way thinking, positive ideas, new imagination, broadened imagination, possibilities, courage to ase your dreams, to overcome the fear of failure through his divine strength.

natever you believe is what you become. If you see yourself successful in your mind, you l be successful in life. Everything starts from the mind, that's why it is important to have a newed mind. A renewed mind is a positive mind that see's life positively irrespective of his esent situation.

DAY 6

(Positive Confession)

1. I am blessed, I think like Christ.
2. My name shall be made Great.
3. My seed is blessed, my children are blessed.
4. I am blessed in the morning, in the noon and in the night.
5. My blessing shall not turn to curse.
6. I cannot be cursed, no curses in my linage, I belong to Christ's linage.
7. I carry eternal blessings.
8. My heart and my mind are renewed. I cannot be limited to my background.
9. I am blessed physically, spiritually, financially, materially, and mentally.
10. I have spiritual treasures and an inheritance in Christ, Jesus is my Guaranto

CHAPTER 7

Beware of Negative People

ere's a saying that says show me your friends and I will tell you who you are. This might und funny, but it is true, whether we like it or not our company determines a lot about the ay we live our lives. The kind of people you move with has a direct or indirect influence on your life and the way you see things. Your company, friends and family have a way of luencing your life. This influence could be either positive or negative.

e scripture tells us of the story of the children of Israel when they sent spies to spy on the d of Canaan. The scripture says in (Numbers 13:1) that God spoke to Moses, saying nd men to spy out the land of Canaan, which I am giving to the children of Israel, so they nt forth men one from each tribe, after forty days the spies returned to Moses and the ngregation with a bad report except for Joshua and Caleb.

w the spies broke into two camps, the camp of negative reporters and the positive porters. The negative camp told Moses; indeed, the land does flow with milk and honey, d this is the fruit however, the people who dwell in the land are strong, the cities are rtified and very large, moreover we saw the descendants of Anak who are huge like ants. I notice that all they could see were reasons why they won't be able to take the land.

ost people only see the problems and challenges, if people around you are those who only e problems and one thousand reasons you shouldn't chase your dreams and visions, it's nes to change friends. The camp of the bad reporters is very good at analysing and scribing problems without solutions. They are experts at analysing ways your ideas will t work instead of thinking of how to help you find a way out.

In verse 31 of Numbers 13, "But the men who had gone up with him said, we are not able go up against the people, for they are stronger than we. They gave the people of Israel bad report of the land. These bad reporters describe the problems they saw in the land a weaken the spirit of the people. There are people like these everywhere, when you sha your ideas with them, they will say it's impossible and give you a thousand ways your id won't work.

They are experts at discouraging people, and they will use words like be 'realistic', they v then tell you many people who has tried it and failed. Be careful to choose your friends a those who you share your dreams and visions with. Be careful of pessimistic people wh have no dreams, no drive, and who use their words to kill other people's dreams and vision

Every time God wants to set a person up for greatness, there are people the devil also war use to get them to doubt God. Most of the times they are close to you, for Joseph it was h brothers. They told him to keep quiet and not talk about his dreams, but he kept dreaming, then he had bigger dreams again and again. Every time they try to keep you sh dream more.

Day 7

I am a child of destiny; I am destined for greatness.

I will fulfil destiny in the name of Jesus.

No power of the enemy can stop me from fulfilling my destiny.

Jesus fulfilled his destiny; I will fulfil mine.

I am possessing my possession; fear of failure will not stop me.

I am above every opposition, No one can stop me.

Joseph was a destiny child, his destiny was fulfilled, my destiny will see the light of day.

My destiny shall not be truncated because of lack of faith. I believe God and I will fulfil my destiny.

My destined shall not be terminated.

. God's plan for my life shall not fail. I will not fail God; I will not fail myself.

CHAPTER 8

Walk with the Wise

Walking with the wise is very important because he who walks with the wise shall al become wise. He who keeps company with the fool will also become a fool. "He who wal with the positive minded will become positively minded and he who chooses to walk with th negatively minded will also become negatively minded".

(Numbers 13:30) says that Caleb quieted the people before Moses and said let us go up once and take possession for we are well able to overcome it. The camp of the go reporters quickly quieted the negative sayers and spoke with courage into the heart of th people, but again the negative camp said we are not able to go up against the people Canaan.

There was tension in the camp, as both parties battled, majority said it is not possible, b Joshua and Caleb still stood their grounds. The truth is that every time you declare positi things the negative always wants to contest with your positive declaration. This is a battle the mind that we will have to fight for the rest of our lives, everyday there's an oppositi against you physically, financially, and spiritually.

This is a battle we fight every day to either stay positive or negative. God wants us to st positive irrespective of what we are going through. He knows that things are not always th way we want but still God wants you to believe in him and have faith. He can turn thin around for your favour.

Walk with the right people who can inspire you positively, listen and read book that kee you challenged to chase your dreams and God's purpose for your life. Your circle of frien s a direct or indirect influence on your lives. It is important to have a spiritual mentor who n help you with divine direction. You need people who can rebuke you when you are ing off the trail.

alk with the wise and you shall be wise, walk with people with good visions and dream, get spired to change your world for good. Don't join the group of complainers, like the children Israel who complained against God, be like Joshua and Caleb (Numbers14:7b), they said e passed through to spy the land and it is an exceedingly good land. Can you say like shua and Caleb we are able to take on the giants and receive that which God has already en us.

(Positive Confession)

1. It's my time to reign, my time to command and rule.
2. I take territories, the nations of the world are opened unto me.
3. I receive grace to succeed and take new territories.
4. I am not a local champion.
5. I am going to the world; the world shall hear me.
6. The earth is the lord and the fulness thereof, I rule my world.
7. I speak things into existence, I create what I want around me.
8. I re-claim lost generational territories.
9. I have been given dominion over the earth. I have dominion.
10. I exercise my Dominion and authority over territories.

CHAPTER 9

Be Courageous

any are afraid to boldly declare God's promises because they fear what other people might
nk and say about them. As children of God, it is essential that we understand the power
d mystery of courageousness. Your level of courage is directly related to what you say
d the way you talk. "You will never rise above the level of your courage." You will never
ercome what you fear until you overcome your fears. Fear paralyses you from taking
tion.

u can tell if people are speaking from fear or from courage. God wants us to speak and
t with courage when we are faced with challenging situation. God doesn't want us to
eak and live in fear. You need to learn how to act boldly.

nen Caleb quieted the spies who gave a negative report, that was an act of courage and
ldness, immediately he said we can take the land for our possession, he gave courage to
ose who had been held by fear. So many people are driven by fear, but it is the wish of
d that we live above our fears.

ar makes you speak negative words, so many people become overwhelmed by their
uation and allow their fears to get the best of them. Once fear gets into the human mind, it
akes the mind to speak and act cowardly. At some point the spies said we were like
asshopper in our own sight, so we were in their sight.

ar basically reduced them to the extent that they saw themselves as small as a
asshopper in their own sight and in the sight of the descendants of Anak. Fear reduces a

person in their mind, but courage does the opposite, courage basically makes you bigg than your fears. No matter how big your fears maybe if you allow God spirit to give boldnes those fears will be driven away.

Watch what people say when they are faced with challenges and problems, then you can what they made of. The holy spirit is the spirit of boldness, the scripture tells us in the Act Apostles (2:14) that Peter and John who were afraid became bold the moment they we filled with the holy spirit. They began to preach boldly and suddenly they were no long scared of been arrested and thrown in the prison.

Be bold, speak boldly, decree and declare God's promises for your life. When you spe boldly you activates God's power for supernatural things. Joshua and Caleb bold declarati gave them the promised land. Peter and John preached with boldness and three thousa souls were won in one day, that is the effect of boldness, boldness always moves the ha of God.

I am experiencing the bold declaration of many years ago now; they are manifesting in r life today. Bold declaration is different from proud talk, it is confessing your faith in God. Yo bold confessions mixed with faith produces miracles above your imaginations.

(2 Tim 1:7) "God has not given us a spirit of fear, but of power and love and of a sound min Fear is not from God, you have power to act during fear, remember courage is not t absence of fear but it is the ability to act in the face of your fears. You have a sound mi and love to stand against every fear.

DAY 9

(Positive Confession)

1. This battle shall not see my end, I shall win.
2. The word of God is working for me.
3. I believe whatever God has said concerning my life.
4. I am bold, fear will not overtake me.
5. I am courageous, I succeed where others failed.
6. God's promises shall come to pass in my life.
7. I have the spirit of Power and love and of a sound mind.
8. Fear shall not paralyse me, I have courage.
9. God's word heals me, delivers me from destruction.
10. The fear of failure will not stop me. I am bold as a lion.

CHAPTER 10

SPEAKING GOD'S WAY

Speaking God's way should be the lifestyle of every child of God. Firstly, every child of God should take after God their father in all ways, especially when it comes to talking. Life is full of challenges and oppositions that makes many people fall in depression, frustration and even forcing some people into the thought of committing suicide.

How do we deal with these critical issues in our society today, as a Christian we are not exempted from daily challenges and opposition. As children of God, we have an obligation to speak like Christ and not speak the way the worldly people speak. Why, because we must acknowledge our dependency is on God, so we must speak with this revelation that God's grace is sufficient for us.

Speak differently because our faith is in the sustainer of the heavens and earth. So therefore, we must speak what God is saying about every situation that we find ourselves. The scripture is a compilation of God's promises for any situation you might find ourselves.

The scripture is like a bunch of keys that you can use to open different doors. When you are facing trials and temptation the scripture is the answer. When you are in the prison of ignorance, the word of God is the key to set you free. When you find yourself in the shackles of sickness the word of God is your healer.

The scripture says "He sent his word and healed them and delivered them from the destructions (Psalm 107:20). The scripture has the solution to any problem that has a name

e issue with Christians is that we can be lazy in searching the word of God that holds the swer to our problems.

your marriage, your health, and your finance is failing, don't be troubled, don't start eaking negatively. Ask yourself a question, what would Jesus do in these circumstances, at would Jesus say? How would Jesus react in this situation? When you search the riptures, you will find the answers and that's the solution to your problem.

hen Jesus was tempted to turn stones to bread after his forty days fasting, Jesus also oted the scripture to the devil from (Deuteronomy 8:3b) "man shall not live by bread alone t by every word that comes from the mouth of God. This shows that Jesus was more rious about God's word more than anything. Jesus was saying that "the quality of the word God you know determines the quality of your spiritual growth." The way you need food for ur physical body is the same way you need God's word for your spiritual body.

sus compared God's word with food which means that, as food is important to the growth the physical body so is the word of God to our spiritual body. You will never grow in the irit without the word of God. If Jesus spoke in God's way, we must learn to speak God's ay to every situation. Jesus believed every bit of God's word, once God said it, it is done.

Day 10

(Positive Confession)

1. The word of God is powerful, Quick and Sharp, I have the word of God livin in me.
2. The lord is my light and my salvation, I cannot be afraid.
3. Fear will not nullify my faith.
4. I am not afraid to step into new territories.
5. Fear of failure cannot stop me from launching out.
6. God is for me, who can be against me.
7. Greater is he that is in me, than he that is in the world.
8. I am courageous, I have power over fears.
9. Christ has conquered all my fears. I am fearless.
10. I am soldier of Christ; I am not a coward; I win all my battles.

CHAPTER 11

TRUE WORSHIP

hat is truly worthy of your worship? Who is truly worthy of your worship? Worship is not st about singing in church, worship is more than just dancing, worship should be a lifetime signment, our lives should bring glory to God every day, everywhere and every time.

any Christians use their tongues in speaking and declaring Gods in church but once they e outside the church environment, they start speaking like the people of the world, hence pping the hand of God from moving in their lives.

me people don't get the result of their declarations because Jesus Christ is no longer the ntre of their lives. Once Jesus Christ is not the centre of your life, there is no power to ck up your words. Don't just seek Christ because of what Christ has to offer, don't run er the gifts but seek to know the giver of the gifts.

orship is from the WORTH, what is worthy of your time, what is worthy of your resources, nat do you invest most of your life and resources on, that's what you are worshipping. You n be a Christian but still not worshipping God or still be an idol worshipper.

u might be wondering how that is possible. If you are Christian and you can do without udying the word of God, prayer, worship, and fellowship but you can't do without your ork, food, mobile phones, and social media. These clearly proves what is worth your time d where you are investing your time and resources. Unknowingly many Christians become ol worshippers of the social world.

Ask yourself how your Christian life is doing? Are you growing or stagnant? Do you think y are getting closer to God or to the world. Whatever you place above God in your life h become your idol. Do you think God is still first in your life. Many Christians have reduc the power of God's word in their lives today because they lost their worship and intima with God.

(John 4:22-24) "You worship what you do not know, but the hour is coming, and is now he when the true worshippers will worship the father in spirit and truth, for the father is seeki such people to worship him. God is a spirit and those who worship him must worship in sp and truth.

For us to see the manifestation of God's glory and power, we must strive to make God t centre of our lives. When you put God first in your life, God will always come through for y in times of battles and trials. (Matt 6:33). God's word in the mouth of a God lover is powerfu

Worship is a lifestyle that involves you putting God first before anyone or anything in th world. It is not easy to worship God truly because we have created idols that have taken t place of God in our lives. The closer you are to God, the more you know God, the best w to know God is to know God's mind and God's mind is revealed through his word.

If you have not given your life to Christ, or you have lost your relationship with him, it's tir to give your to Christ and make God first in your life. Please say this prayer "Lord Jesus believe you died for me and that God Almighty raised you from the dead. Please forgive my sins. I choose to turn away from them now and I ask you to come into my heart as r lord and saviour".

DAY 11

(Positive Confession)

1. Lord, I lay down my Idols, Lord, take your place in my life.
2. Whatever is occupying God's space in my life be removed.
3. Voice of self-doubt be silence in my life.
4. Idols will not take God's place in my life.
5. Self-doubt will not stop me from acting on God's word.
6. Voice of unbelief, trying to draw me away from Christ be silenced.
7. I have great faith; Christianity is working for me.
8. My worship is renewed for God and God alone.
9. No more idol worshipping.
10. I am for Christ; heaven is my goal.

CHAPTER 12

IT IS POSSIBLE

A positive mindset produces a positive confession. A negative mind will also produ negative confession. A mango tree will never produce an apple tree, a man will only spe what he has on the inside. The foundation of positive confession is directly connected your mindset. A person with a possibility mindset will always see challenges differently.

God wants us to declare and speak differently, how you see life matters. Your minds determines how you will approach challenges and problems in life. For most people wh they are faced with challenges, they withdraw back and accept their current status wh others see challenges as a normal part of life, and they face it squarely.

God wants you to trust and hope in him. Why is it important to trust in God? Because God the un-sustained sustainer of all living things in heaven and on earth. He alone is r sustained by anything or anyone. God is the uncreated creator of all things, nothing w made without him, he is the foundation of all things visible and invisible. God is the only o that cannot fail, he cannot make mistake. He sees the begin and know the end, He is call the alpha and the omega.

Nothing is too hard for God to do, nothing is impossible to him, only God is worthy of o trust and hope. No other person or power is worthy of your trust because they were create and they are limited in capacity. Only God remains the unlimited one, he can't be limited time or space, he lives outside of time and space. He knows the end from the beginning.

e scripture says "for with God nothing will be impossible ". God specialises in doing things at man can never phantom. God wants us to believe that he can do anything, he wants us declare his word to those challenges, that he is able to do all things. If God has promised u something big and it's yet to manifest in your life, I urge you to believe God because he able to do it.

ep believing and declaring God's word concerning your life especially when you are going ough a tough time, sometimes we are trying to work it out with our limited brain. The truth that man's brain is too small to search or understand God's way.

aiah 55:8-9) "for my thoughts are not your thoughts says the lord, neither are my ways ur ways declare the lord, for as the heavens are higher than the earth, so are my ways. All ngs are possible to them that believe. (Mark 9:23). God will always work and do raculous things, don't try to figure everything out. Just believe in God, whatever you are king for is possible.

DAY 12

(Positive Confession)

1. Every spiritual covering of darkness, covering my eyes be removed.
2. Every veil covering my eyes from seeing possibility be removed now.
3. My eyes be opened to see possibility, breakthroughs, creative idea, and innovation
4. My eyes be opened to see solutions and divine revelations.
5. The eyes of my mind be opened, unbelief will not stop me.
6. My eyes are the eyes of Christ, I see abundance, Miracles, and open doors.
7. My eyes are empowered to see success, Favor, and Glory.
8. I am anointed to see solution, possibility, and opportunities.
9. All things are possible for me, I always make it.
10. I believe in God's destiny and plan for my life.

CHAPTER 13

I CAN DO ALL THINGS

hatever God has called you to do, he has provided the strength to do them through Christ sus. (Philippians 4:13) "I can do all things through Christ which strengthens me. Paul was nfident in God's divine strength, and he was able to leverage on Christ strength to achieve eat things. Most people struggle in life because they only rely on their human ability.

ul understood that for you to succeed in life you need God's strength. There's nothing that n stop you from succeeding and fulfilling destiny if you leverage on God's divine strength. d wants us to declare like Paul, irrespective of our weaknesses and shortcomings. He nts to declare positively, Paul understood that by his own power he was limited so he ned to Christ divine strength to do all things.

hatever challenges you are going through, know that God wants us to boldly declare his ength. You are not alone; you have been empowered and enabled to withstand any thing e enemies throw at you.

e problem is that we concentrate on our problems too much that we magnify our problems the extent that we reduce the power of God in us. Every time you magnify your problems u reduce God's strength in your life. Am not asking you to deny you have problems, it is rmal to have a problem if you are on planet earth, you will have a direct or indirect oblem. Don't let your problem get a hold of you to drag you into depression, complaining d murmuring against God.

Some people are so focused on what is not working in their lives, they forget to see other things that is working for them. You have a lot working for you than what is not working you. Quit the pity party, it will only worsen your mental health condition. Remember, the t spies who went to spy the land of Canaan, they magnified their enemies so much that the reduced themselves to the size of a grasshopper.

Listen, when you change your focus from the problem and you accept God's strength, t power of God automatically kicks in and turns that same problem to an opportunity for you lifting. David used the same principle to overcome Goliath.

Goliath was nine feet and nine inches tall, and David was 5 feet tall, Goliath was a traine warrior and the champion of the Philistines army, David was a shepherd boy. Howeve David did not look at Goliath height or his special military rank, he reduced Goliath in h mind and magnified the God of Israel.

David said I come against you in the name of the lord, I shall give you head to birds of th air. Wow, imagine that confidence to face a giant. The bible says, the name of the lord is strong tower, the righteous run into it and they are saved. (Proverbs 18:10).

Physically speaking Goliath was bigger, fearful, and more powerful, but David leveraged o God's divine strength. David knew Goliath was nothing compared to the size of his God. H brought Goliath down with just a stone, one stone backed up with God's strength ende Goliath as big as he was, because he already minimised Goliath to nothing. He magnifie God above the problem. Stop magnifying your problems and watch God turn those problem into opportunities for your celebration.

DAY 13

(Positive Confession)

1. I refuse to be ignorant of God's strength available to me.
2. I align my spirit to take delivery of God's promises for my life.
3. I receive my divine transformation.
4. I walk into God's promises for my victory.
5. I refuse to magnify my problems; my problems turn to opportunities.
6. I am empowered and enabled to do all things through Christ strength.
7. I magnify God above every problem.
8. I am empowered by God to slay giants and win generational battles.
9. I step out of doubt to receive God's promises for my life.
10. I access divine grace and strength to take delivery of whatever God has promised me by faith.

CHAPTER 14

GIVE YOUR ANGELS SOMETHING TO WORK WITH

Whatever you say is like a seed you are sowing. If you sow a seed, be prepared for harvest because its coming, so make sure you are sowing the right seeds into your future. God revealed to me in (Psalm 91:11). "For he shall give his angels charge over you, to keep you in all your ways".

Every child of God has angels around them, most people are not aware of this secret. There are angels that protects you like bodyguards, God has given his angels commands to be with you, not only to protect you, but they are also carry out your command and instructions.

You cannot afford to be a careless talker, remember they carry out your commands, so if you are saying negative things continually your angels will make sure you get what you are asking for eventually. Most people have been speaking negative words, unknowing to them when they say negative words, they just come to pass in their lives.

One day while I was meditating on the word, God dropped a revelation into my mind that many Christians are not giving their angels something to work with. Some are giving their angels the negative words to work with. God dropped this question into my mind "What are you giving your angels to work with". If God was to open our eyes, many would be surprised with the numbers of angels around them.

In the book of 2 kings 6:16 Elisha said to his servant Don't be afraid "those who are with us are more than those who are with them. Then he prayed to God to open his servants' eyes and he looked and saw the hills full of angels with horses and chariots of fire all around isha. Many Christians are carrying around a host of angels unknowing to them because eir eyes are not opened.

hen you begin to speak the right words and declare God's word, it puts your angels to ork, you send them on errands and give them orders. Start decreeing, speak the word, ere is no barrier in the spirit realm, the angels can hear you. Say what you want and keep ving your angels something to work with.

DAY 14

(Positive Confession)

1. Every mindset that is not of God. Be uprooted from my life.
2. My angels are working on my behalf. They are bringing all that I have commanded me.
3. I command my angels to be on guard. I am protected.
4. I decree my angels to deliver my blessing, my favour, my increase.
5. I am not small; I am a giant in the spirit.
6. I am not poor, I am rich, poverty is uprooted from my life.
7. Christ already took my sickness; I am healed by his stripes.
8. I am not weak, I am strong.
9. I am blessed, no more curses in my life. I have generation blessings in Christ Jesus
10. Failure at the edge of my breakthrough is not my portion.

CHAPTER 15

THE WORD IS A LIGHT

ou need light to overcome darkness around you. Anywhere darkness reigns, there is ways chaos and confusion but when the light shines, darkness must disappear. The :ripture says in Psalm (119:105) "Your word is a lamp to my feet and a light to my path. Do ɔu know why many people are lost in life? It's because they lost the light of God. They do ɔt have the word of God in their life, talk less of using the word of God to change their lives.

nce the word of God is lost from a person's heart and mouth, the person automatically falls to darkness and lost their direction. They wander off the path of life, that's why the :riptures says (Joshua 1:8) "This book of the law shall not depart from your mouth, but you nall meditate in it day and night, that you may observe to do according to all that is written it, for then you will make your way prosperous and then you will have good success.

od has clearly given man a formular for success in every sphere of life. God delivered a inciple for us to live by if we want to succeed God's way. Firstly, never let the word of God epart from your mouth. Listen, your mouth must keep speaking the word of God to confront ny challenge that comes your way. Challenges comes in different forms, and everyone has challenge whether poor or rich, everyone has his own problems.

ɔu must keep speaking to yourself positively irrespective of your present status don't stop eclaring what God says about you. Don't join the group of complainers and the pity party here all they do is discuss how things are not working, how hard the economy is. Don't join e crowd, stand-out and be different.

Mediate on God's word day and night, make it a priority to think about God's word and act on his word. Think on the word in the day and in the night once you receive a revelation act on it. You are sure to succeed when you apply God's principles of speaking, mediating, and acting by faith. The word of God is dynamic, it can address any kind of problem or challenge you find yourself. Make use of God's word and your life will experience a positive shift.

DAY 15

(Positive Confession)

1. I have the mind of God in me.
2. The old mindset that has limited me is removed now.
3. I decree my mind is renewed; I am a new creature.
4. Darkness is out of my life; I have the light of God.
5. Mind set of impossibility give way to possibility.
6. Mindset of limitation be removed.
7. Mindset of mediocrity is replaced with excellence mindset.
8. Poverty mindset be replaced with the mindset of wealth.
9. I can never be poor; I can never be sick in Jesus' name.
10. I have a success mindset because I have the light of God around me.

CHAPTER 16

QUICK AND POWERFUL

od's word is a powerful weapon against the devil and his craft. Many Christians have lost
ome battles in life because of their ignorance of the word of God. The devil fears anyone
ith a deep understanding of the word of God. The scripture says in (Hebrews 4:12) "For the
ord of God is quick, and powerful, and sharper than any two-edged sword, piercing even to
e dividing asunder of soul and spirit, and of the joints and marrow, and is a discerner of the
oughts and intent of the heart".

e scripture compares the word of God with a sword, because it's a weapon of attack and
efence for the Christians in time of trouble. In our days, I would liken the word of God with
e most powerful nuclear weapon in the world. God intentionally gave us his word to act as
shield of defence from the devil and temptations.

e word of God is so powerful, that is the only thing the devil respects. The scripture says
(John 1:1). In the beginning was the word and the word was with God and the word was
od. God is equal to his word, God's power is equal to the power of the word, the more you
ut God's word into use the bigger your success.

e word is quick, it acts immediately it's sent. (Mark 11:12-25). Jesus was hungry, seeing in
e distance a fig tree in leaf, he went to find out if it had any fruit. When he reached it, he
und nothing but leaves, because it was not the season for figs. In Verse 14, Then Jesus
aid to the tree "May no one ever eat fruit from you again." And the disciples heard him say
 In the morning as they went along, they saw the fig tree withered from the roots. Peter
aid to Jesus, Rabbi look, the tree you cursed has withered.

Jesus exercised power through his word over the tree. The moment he spoke the tree withered it was just a matter of time for the physical manifestation. The word of God work immediately and manifest with time in the physical realm. So, if you have been genuine decreeing and declaring the word, very soon you will see a manifestation in the physic world.

When you have the word of God in you, you become a dangerous soldier that the dev fears. Remember, Jesus overcame his temptation by using the word of God. The word God in your mouth is as powerful as it is in God's mouth. God's word is supreme ove everything visible and invisible.

DAY 16

(Positive Confession)

1. The word of God is working wonders in my life.
2. I am becoming like Jesus Christ in my actions.
3. God is transforming me into his son's image of glory.
4. Whatever cannot stop Jesus, cannot stop me.
5. Whatever worked out for Jesus is working for me.
6. I am a new creature in Christ, old things have passed away.
7. Look at me, all things have become new.
8. I think like Jesus, I am unstoppable.
9. I talk like Jesus, I speak possibility.
10. I walk like Jesus; I can do all things through Christ.

CHAPTER 17

THE WORD TRANSFORMS

In life you are going to experience a lot of challenges, but there's one power that can change your situation however bad it may be, the word of God. Believing and speaking the word God can bring you out of pain, sickness, sin, frustration, and hopelessness. There's nothir you are going through that is more powerful than the word of God.

God's word can uproot what the enemy has planted in your life (Hebrews 4:12). God's wo is the only thing that can change and transform our spirit, soul, and the body. Romans 12 "Don't copy the behaviour and the customs of this world, but let God transform you into new person by changing the way you think. Then you will learn to know God's will for yo which is good and pleasing, and perfect."

The truth is that as Christians we are not exempted from troubles in this world, wh differentiates us is that Christ has promised us victory. As a child of God, you need to spea differently, don't talk like the people who have no God, don't copy, and behave like them. L God's word transform you from inside out. Think, speak, and act on God's word.

 Let the word of God turn you into a new person by renewing your mind through the word God. Don't let what you are going through have you. You may have pains, but don't let th pains have you, you can have sickness, but don't let that sickness have you. The scripture say in Psalm 30:5b, weeping may endure for a night, but joy comes in the morning.

God is reassuring us that whatever we may be passing through is not the end for us. Th problem won't see your end, that depression won't see your end, that poverty won't see yo nd, that pain and sickness won't see your end. You may be in the nighttime of your life here you weep in secret, don't give up, your morning is coming. Joy is on the way, you hall rejoice.

ome years ago, I was led by God to apply for my masters in the United Kingdom. During e processing period I encountered a lot of setback and rejection, I was refused three times the space of seven years, but I held unto God's word, eventually after many years of ying, nights of prayers, fasting, weeping and seed sacrifice, God finally showed up.

was finally given the visa, all those who have mocked me and written me off were sappointed. I pray for someone who has been experiencing a disappointment in any area, ay the lord who changed my story change your story and make you smile again.

DAY 17

(Positive Confession)

1. I decree a shift a from victim to victor.
2. I decree my night season is over, my morning season is here.
3. I shift from nothing to something.
4. I move from sickness to perfect health.
5. I change levels, I enter my next level.
6. Evil patterns in my life are broken in Jesus' name.
7. I enter my glory; I enter the season of the manifestation of my destiny.
8. My change is supernatural, I cannot be stagnated in Jesus' name.
9. I am moving higher and higher, upwards ever.
10. Disappointments is over from my life.

CHAPTER 18

You must Believe

od cannot change your situation until you believe. Faith is important for your expectation to
e a reality. Your faith is the key to the manifestation of your miracle. Matt 9:28b "Jesus
sked the blind man that came to him, do you believe that I am able to do this? Yes, lord,
ey replied, then he touched their eyes and said, according to your faith let it be done to
ou, and their sight was restored. The issues we are struggling with most times can be
aced to our lack of faith.

Jesus should say to most people "Let it be done to you according to your faith", many still
ould not have their miracle because they lack faith. Mark 6:5 "He could not do any miracles
ere, except laying his hands on a few sick people and heal them. Jesus marvelled because
 their unbelief, then he went about the village in a circuit teaching. Can you imagine that
sus couldn't help this village as much as he wanted because of their unbelief.

nbelief de-actives God's power. Do you believe that God's promises can be fulfilled in your
e? Do you have faith for your dream of travelling the world, do you believe your dream of
ing an entrepreneur or whatever you wish is possible? Do you believe you can be healed?
o you believe you can be rich?

od cannot help you until you believe. Faith activates the power of God, your faith in God
leases the grace of God. Faith activates God strength in you even our salvation comes by
ace through faith. (Hebrews 11:1) "Now faith is the substance of things hoped for the
vidence of things not seen. So, faith means that you believe in the existence of something
ven though you can't see it in the physical.

The problem with many people is that they want to see it first before they believe its real. Some Christians won't believe they are rich until they see the money in their account, that where they have the challenge. You don't have to wait to see it before you believe because until you can see it in your mind, you won't see it in your life, that's God's way.

The scripture says in 2 Cor 4:18 that "while we do not look at the things which are seen but at the things which are unseen" for the things which are seen are temporary but the thing which are not seen are eternal. Whatever situation you are facing today is only temporary. better day is coming for you.

That problem you have today is temporary, you must believe you are blessed, because God said it. If you believe it, you will see it, whatever has not entered your mind cannot enter you life. If God has said, that settles it.

MK11:24 says Therefore I tell you, whatever you ask for in prayer, believe that you have received it, and it will be yours. Some are praying and asking God for a miracle they don believe or expect. You will never experience a miracle until what you are asking for is equal to what you believe in your heart.

The scripture says, believe you have received it and then it will be yours. Many times, we want to believe God only when we have received it but that is not the formular. Believe firs act like you have received it, speak like you have it already, get it in your mind and then it will be yours.

DAY 18

(Positive Confession)

1. My faith is strong, I believe I am a success, and I will succeed.
2. I activate God's power for miracles in my life.
3. Spirit of Doubt, go out of my life.
4. My dream shall come true.
5. I believe I am blessed; I cannot be cursed.
6. I believe I am healed; sickness cannot rule in my life.
7. I am highly blessed and favoured.
8. By faith, I am manifesting God's glory.
9. I am who God says I am, I have what God says I have.
10. I decree my needs are met; I live in abundance.

CHAPTER 19

Be Patient

Patience is one of the important virtues that you will need as a child of God however, this missing in the life of many people. Most people just want it now or never, they want the dreams and goals to be achieved quickly. The scripture teaches us to learn how to b patient, how to wait on the lord. If you say you have faith in God, you must be able to wait o God for the fulfilment of your destiny.

Destiny cannot be microwaved; you must learn patience. Lack of patience is dangerous the fulfilment of your dreams. The inability to wait on God shows our lack of confidence ar lack of absolute trust in God. Very often we are faced with challenges, and we tend to act o of impatience, risking our life and destiny, and that of others too.

Many believers behave like non-believers when they go ahead of God when seeking for Jo opportunities, careers, marriage, and by the time they realise it was a wrong move then the start seeking for God. It is better to afford regret by always seeking divine direction and th grace for patience. Many people cannot stay on a dream to see it grow before jumping un another one.

Patience is the ability to wait for the fulfilment of God's purpose in our lives. The ability stay on one vision, like Noah, Abraham. Don't leave God outside of your life because yc can't wait for his direction. 1 Samuel (13:5-13). When the Israelites were to gather for batt against the philistines, King Saul was commanded to wait seven days for Samuel to retu and officiate the worship, before the end of the seven days king Saul went ahead to perfor the worship ceremony, he couldn't wait because of impatience. This act of impatienc caused king Saul to lose the kingdom as God became angry with him.

earn to wait on the lord, Isaiah 40:31, but those who wait on the lord shall renew their trength, they shall mount up with wings of eagles, they shall run and not be weary, they nall walk and not faint. If you believe God, you will be patient. If God has said it, then it is ettled, don't settle for less because of impatience. (Hebrews 11:7) "By faith Noah built the rk at age 500 and flood did not come until he was 600 years of age. He was patient for 100 ears to wait for God's promise. Devil wants you to doubt God and lose the reward of atience.

ou must learn to stand on God's word and wait for God's time. Patience is the ability to hold nto a position and wait for God's instruction. Sometimes that position will not be omfortable or pleasant for you, but God knows the future. Patience is the ability to declare od's promises when the situation looks hopeless. Imagine the people mocking Noah while e was building the boat and waiting for rain, People mocked Abraham while he was waiting r a child at his old age. If people are mocking you today because of God's promise on life, st be patient and very soon God is going to show up for you. If men have not mocked you, od cannot make you. Look unto Jesus the author and finisher of our faith.

DAY 19

1. I am patient, I will wait on the lord till my help comes.
2. Impatience will not destroy my destiny.
3. As I wait on the lord, my strength is renewed every day.
4. I will not lose God's promise because of impatience.
5. My shame is gone, God is making me.
6. My testimony is sure, God is working things for my good.
7. All things are working for my good.
8. I serve the sufficient God; I live in abundance.
9. I will walk and not faint, I will run and not be weary.
10. God word cannot fail, God's word won't fail in my life.

CHAPTER 20

BE JOYFUL ALWAYS

ou must be joyful no matter what you are going through. Joyfulness is not the absence of attles or problem; joyfulness is a command from God to his children. One of the ways you ill know a child of God is through the spirit of joy in them. (Habakkuk 3:17-19) "Though the eery tree does not blossom, and the strawberries does not ripen, though the apples are orm-eaten, and the wheat fields stunted, though the sheep pens are sheepless and the attle barns empty, yet I will sing joyful praise to God". This scripture is so amazing that we ust learn from it that our joy should not be tied to the outcome of things around us.

ven if you are failing and everything fails, God wants you to remain joyful. Your business ay not be working, you may be struggling with your academics, your health may be failing, our marriage may be at the edge of falling, close friends and family abandoned you, God ays still be joyful. Logically when things are not going well, we tend to feel sad, and heart oken. The scripture in Habakkuk 3:17-19 tell us that everything went bad for Habakkuk, it he never allowed it to take his joy.

ost people withdraw their praise and even blame God at the slightest disappointment they xperience. Some people stop praying, some even don't want to hear about God because ings are not working the way they want it. (Job 13:15a) "Even though he kills me, I will ope in him. This man lost everything but never lost his hope in God. In (Job 42:10) The cripture says the lord restored the fortune of Job twice than before. If Job had committed icide when this were bad for him, he would have never lived to see everything he lost stored in double folds.

ome out of your depression and sorrow, whatever you have lost will be restored if you keep our joy in the lord. Habakkuk decided to be joyful during his hard time and trusted God for his salvation. He continued to praise God and confessed positively with faith. Whenever you are struggling and facing challenges don't let it steal your joy, choose to rejoice in the lord.

Don't get frustrated, angry, depressed, and moody instead turn it around and give praise God. When you rejoice in the lord, it proves that your faith and confidence is in him. Listen nothing activates God power of restoration more than praise and joyfulness. (Philippians 4:4 "Rejoice in the lord always and again I say rejoice. God wants us to rejoice in him every time irrespective of what we are going through.

The scripture says in Act 16:25, but at midnight when Paul and Silas were praying and singing hymns of praise to God, and the prisoners were listening to them, suddenly there was a great earthquake so powerful that the foundation of the prison were shaken and once all the doors were opened and everyone's chain was broken. There's power in your praise, be joyful always, let your joy be in the salvation of God.

DAY 20

(Positive Confession)

1. Nothing can steal my joy from me.
2. The joy of the lord is my strength.
3. No matter what I face, I will rejoice in the lord always.
4. As God restored Job, I shall have my restoration.
5. I am blessed and highly favoured.
6. Whatever is not working in my life, as I praise God begin to work.
7. I refuse to be frustrated; I have the joy of the lord.
8. I shall not go into depression, I come out of mourning, and I enter joy.
9. I rejoice always, no time for sadness.
10. I am joyful, thankful, and always grateful.

CHAPTER 21

ACT ON THE WORD

Nothing will change in your life until you decide to move. A body at rest will remain at rest until a force is applied. Force is required to change the status of an object, for your destiny to enter manifestation you need to act on what God has told you. Many destines are stranded because they refuse to act, without action your dreams will remain in a dream state forever. After you have received God's word either through the scriptures or through divine revelation, you need to act boldly without fear.

(James 2:18) "But someone may say, you claim to have faith and I have good works, show me your faith without works, I will show you my faith by my works". If you claim to have faith your faith should show by your action. If you pray and do all the positive confessions but do not act on what you have prayed and believed for, there will be no result or manifestation of miracles. (Hebrews 11:7) "By faith Noah moved with Godly fear to build an ark for saving his household." Noah believed and obeyed God's command irrespective of what the society thinks, whether the people believed or not, Noah acted on God's word.

There is power in action. Stop sitting idle and expecting things to change around you. Don't wait for things to happen, happen to things. Don't just be re-active, be pro-active, make things happen. See God has given you power, strength, and boldness to make changes life and in the world. Your faith without action is useless. (Gen 12:1-4) says God spoke Abram to leave his father's house and God promised him that he will make him great, and Abraham departed as the lord directed him. Listen, if Abram did not move out of his father's house, he wouldn't have become blessed. God didn't even tell him his destiny, still he believed God and left.

If it were most people, some would argue, some would give excuses and some would tell God, let's analyse this trip, they would ask for travel itinerary. Abram just obeyed; he acted on God's word. Stop wasting time and act on the last command God gave you, stop analysing and strategizing without a clear plan of action. What is the benefit of your analysis you are never going to implement the plan.

ew years ago, God told me to relocate from Nigeria to the UK, I didn't have all the resources I needed but I began to move, made enquires on what I needed to do, while working towards it, God provided the resources, it looked impossible at that time but today is a reality. I encountered all kinds of kickbacks and stumbling blocks, but I kept on pushing. Real courage is acting on God's word when things are not going your way.

Don't give up on God (Num 23:19) "God is not a man that he should lie nor a son of man that he should repent, has he said, and will he not do it? Or has he spoken and will he not make good and fulfil it. Hold onto God, lunch out, leave your comfort zone, and possess your possessions. When God speaks, he goes ahead of you. He is the alpha and omega.

The scripture says in Galatians chapter 6 verse 9 "Let us not grow weary or become discouraged in doing good, for at the proper time we will reap, if we do not give in. Don't be weary, don't get discouraged, continue your good work, continue confessing positively and act with courage, in due season you shall harvest your testimony, Joy, favour, financial breakthrough, peace, rest, healing and your restoration.

Don't worry about what you lost, who walked away from your life, how much time you have lost. If you decide to act on God's word, you activate God's divine restoration power. The same God that commanded Ezekiel to prophecy to the dry bones in Ezekiel chapter 37, is commanding you today to prophecy upon your life, speak the word upon that area of your life that is unproductive and not showing forth the glory of God. Prophecy upon your life and you shall experience the power of restoration in the name of Jesus.

(Positive Confession)

1. I refuse to be a lazy Christian.
2. I make things happen; I am a change agent.
3. I am not re-active, I am pro-active.
4. I exterminate the power of procrastination, postponing my miracle.
5. My destiny journey will not be stagnant.
6. I will act on God's word without wasting time.
7. I will not give up on God's word, God's will for my life shall come to pass.
8. Whatever I have lost is restored.
9. I command my dry bones to come back to life.
10. I shall harvest the labour of my hands in due season, my labour shall not be wasted

Think And Speak Positively

ost times we underestimate the power of thought, words, and action. Thought is one of the ost valuable things in the planet. Pastor Solomon Fapohunda believes that there is imaginable power in our thought, words, and action.

very time you say a positive or negative word you are sowing a seed. The scripture says in Proverbs 18:21) Death and life are in the power of the tongue those who love it will eat the uits. This means that everyone shall bear the consequences of your own words.

his 21-days interactive devotional journal immerses you into a positive atmosphere where ou can grasp more understanding of positive speaking and you can begin to see possibility here you have been experiencing difficulties. This devotional will reveal the power of ought, the power of speaking positively and the power of action on God's word.

astor Solomon Fapohunda is the founder, president, and senior pastor of Restoration ssembly ministry UK. He is a young, vibrant preacher and an inspirational speaker. As a peaker he has inspired and empowered many to discover their personal purpose and evelop their true potentials. He and his wife are blessed with two children. He resides in the nited Kingdom.

NOTES

NOTES

NOTES

NOTES

NOTES

NOTES

NOTES

NOTES

NOTES

NOTES

NOTES

NOTES

NOTES

NOTES

Printed in Great Britain
by Amazon